AI CASHFLOW

How to Make Money Online
with AI for Beginners

by Buck Tyler

Disclaimer Notice

Important Information

This book is intended for informational purposes only and should not be considered financial advice. While the book explores various methods for making money online using AI, it is crucial to understand that individual results may vary significantly. The techniques and strategies presented in this book involve inherent risks, and success is not guaranteed.

Please be advised

Investing in any online venture carries inherent risks of financial loss. You should carefully consider your financial situation and risk tolerance before attempting any of the methods described in this book.
The AI landscape is constantly evolving. While the book strives to provide up-to-date information, some techniques or tools mentioned may become outdated or unavailable in the future.
Individual success depends on various factors beyond the scope of this book. These factors include your skills, experience, dedication, market conditions, and even a degree of luck.
It is essential to conduct your own research and due diligence before investing in any AI-related projects or tools mentioned in this book.

By using the information in this book, you acknowledge and agree that you are solely responsible for your own financial decisions and outcomes.

Table of Content

Introduction

Imagine creating captivating artwork with just a few words, writing engaging blog posts in seconds, or composing music tailored to your mood – all thanks to the magic of artificial intelligence. This isn't science fiction; it's the exciting world of generative AI, where machines learn to analyze information and create entirely new things.

But what exactly is generative AI, and how can you leverage its power to make money? Buckle up as we dive into this fascinating field and explore its potential for turning your ideas into profits.

What is Generative AI?

Generative AI, also known as generative models, refers to a specific type of artificial intelligence capable of creating entirely new content, like text, images, code, music, or even 3D models, based on the data it's been trained on. Unlike traditional AI, which is focused on analyzing and understanding existing data, generative AI learns its training data's underlying patterns and structures and goes beyond to produce something original.

Think of it this way: imagine a talented artist who has studied countless paintings throughout their career. They have absorbed different art movements' styles, techniques, and nuances. Now, given a simple prompt like "a vibrant underwater scene," they can create a unique painting that captures the essence of the prompt while incorporating their artistic flair. Generative AI works similarly but on a much larger scale and can quickly process and generate information.

Here's a breakdown of the key aspects of Generative AI:

How it works:

- Training: Generative models are trained on massive datasets of existing content, like text, images, or code. This training allows the model to understand the statistical relationships and patterns within the data.
- Generation: Once trained, the model can be prompted to generate new content with similar characteristics to the data it was trained on. For example, a text-based generative model could be prompted to write a poem in

the style of Shakespeare, or an image-based model could be prompted to create a picture of a cat based on the information it has learned about cats.

- Types of models: There are various generative models, each with strengths and weaknesses. Some common examples include Generative Adversarial Networks (GANs), Variational Autoencoders (VAEs), and Transformer-based models.

Applications:

- Creative content creation: Generative AI is already used for creative applications like writing poems, scripts, musical pieces, or generating unique visual content for marketing materials.
- Drug discovery and material science: Scientists use generative models to discover new drugs and materials by exploring combinations of molecules or properties with desired characteristics.
- Personalization: Generative models can personalize user experiences by recommending products, generating custom content, or translating languages more naturally.
- Data augmentation: Generative models can create synthetic data to supplement real-world data, which is particularly useful for training machine learning models where real data might be scarce or expensive to collect.

Impact and considerations:

- Benefits: Generative AI has the potential to revolutionize various industries by automating tasks, enhancing creativity, and accelerating innovation.
- Challenges: Ethical considerations like bias, copyright infringement, and the potential for misuse are important to address as generative AI evolves.
- Future: As research and development continue, generative AI is poised to become even more powerful and ubiquitous, bringing exciting opportunities and challenges for society.

The Future of Generative AI

The field of generative AI is still in its early stages, but it has the potential to revolutionize many industries. As generative models become more sophisticated and accessible, we expect to see more innovative applications emerge. If you're interested in exploring the creative possibilities of generative AI, now is the perfect time to jump in and start experimenting. With a dash of creativity and a willingness to learn, you can leverage this powerful technology to turn your ideas into reality and potentially make money.

AI Tools that I recommend for Make Money Online

Free Tools:

1. ChatGPT

ChatGPT, for Chat Generative Pre-trained Transformer, is a large language model chatbot developed by OpenAI. Launched in November 2022, it's based on the powerful GPT-3.5 and GPT-4 language models and excels at engaging in conversational interactions.

ChatGPT, with its conversational prowess and text-generation capabilities, finds applications in various domains. Here's a breakdown of some key uses:

Customer Service:

- Answering frequently asked questions: ChatGPT can handle basic inquiries, freeing up human agents for complex issues.
- Providing personalized support: By understanding the context of conversations, it can offer relevant solutions and resources.
- 24/7 availability: It can handle inquiries outside business hours, improving customer satisfaction.

Education:

- Personalized learning: ChatGPT can adapt to individual needs, offering practice questions and explanations in different formats.

- Feedback and assessment: It can provide automated feedback on written work and assess understanding through interactive conversations.
- Engaging content creation: It can create educational materials like quizzes and presentations or even simulate historical figures for interactive learning.

Creative Writing:

- Overcoming writer's block: It can suggest ideas, generate text snippets, or provide different writing styles to inspire creativity.
- Brainstorming and collaboration can be a sounding board for ideas, suggesting different plotlines or character developments.
- Generating different creative formats: It can write poems, scripts, musical pieces, or code snippets based on user prompts.

Entertainment:

- Conversational companion: It can engage in casual conversations, tell jokes, or play text-based games.
- Interactive storytelling can create personalized stories based on user choices and preferences.
- Language learning: It can simulate conversations with native speakers, helping users practice their language skills.

Other Applications:

- Product descriptions and marketing copy can generate unique and engaging product descriptions, marketing materials, or social media posts.
- Data analysis and summarization: It can process large amounts of text data and summarize key findings.
- Code generation and translation: It can generate basic code snippets or translate code between different programming languages.

Suppose your work is related to researching and writing. ChatGPT can help you easily with just your command or ask questions, no matter what type of writing it is. (We call this "prompt").

2. Gemini (Google Bard)

Gemini is a large language model (LLM) named Bard, developed by Google AI. It can be used for:

Creative Writing & Content Generation:

- Brainstorming ideas & overcoming writer's block: Generate different text formats like poems, scripts, musical pieces, emails, letters, etc., based on your instructions.
- Content creation assistance: Write blog posts, product descriptions, marketing copy, and other materials in various styles and tones.
- Personalized stories & interactive experiences: Craft engaging narratives based on user choices and preferences.

Education & Learning:

- Personalized learning experiences: Adapt to individual needs by offering practice questions, explanations, and feedback on written work.
- Interactive learning materials: Generate quizzes presentations, or even simulate historical figures for engaging learning experiences.
- Language learning practice: Simulate conversations with native speakers to help users practice their language skills.

Communication & Customer Service:

- Conversational companion: Engage in casual conversations, tell jokes, or play text-based games.
- Customer service interactions: Answer frequently asked questions, provide personalized support, and offer 24/7 availability.
- Information retrieval & summarization: Process large amounts of text data and summarize key findings.

Productivity & Tools:

- Meeting summaries & note-taking: Generate summaries of meetings and capture key points.
- Code generation & translation: Generate basic code snippets or translate code between different programming languages.
- Email & letter writing assistance: Craft professional emails or personalized letters in different styles and tones.

Like ChatGPT, Gemini can help you write anything you want. Just prompt it.

3. Bing Copilot

Bing Copilot is an AI-powered search and productivity tool by Microsoft. It was launched in February 2023 as "Bing Chat" and rebranded with its current name in September 2023.

Here's a breakdown of Bing Copilot's key features and uses:

What it does:

- Provides comprehensive answers to your questions: Unlike a traditional search engine, Bing Copilot doesn't just list links. It analyzes data from various sources and presents a single, summarized answer tailored to your question.
- Engages in natural conversation: You can ask follow-up questions, clarify your needs, and chat casually with Copilot. It understands the context and responds accordingly.
- Assists with creative tasks: It can write different creative text formats like poems, code, scripts, musical pieces, and even generate images based on your instructions.
- Offers personalized experiences: It considers your search history, preferences, and location to provide relevant suggestions and results.
- Works across devices and contexts: Access Copilot through the Bing website, Microsoft Edge browser, Microsoft 365 applications, and even Windows 11 devices with right-click integration.

Who can use it:

- Anyone with a Microsoft account or Entra ID: Sign up for free to access most features. Paid plans offer additional benefits like priority access and customization options.
- Individuals: Students, writers, researchers, professionals, and anyone looking for an AI-powered assistant for daily tasks.
- Businesses: Marketing teams, customer service representatives, and content creators can leverage Copilot's capabilities for various tasks.

Key highlights:

- Emphasis on privacy and security: Microsoft prioritizes user privacy and offers controls over data usage and personalization.
- Integration with Microsoft ecosystem: Seamlessly works with other Microsoft tools like Office applications and Edge browser.
- Constant improvement: Regularly updated with new features and improved functionalities.

Like ChatGPT and Gemini, Copilot can help you with writing jobs.

Paid Tools

1. Midjourney

Midjourney is a generative AI program and service created by Midjourney, Inc., focused on transforming textual descriptions into captivating visual artworks. Launched in July 2022, it has gained substantial traction in the AI art scene for its accessibility and impressive image quality.

Here's a breakdown of Midjourney's key aspects:

Functionality:

- Turns text prompts into images: Users craft textual descriptions, often called prompts, detailing the desired image content, style, and composition. Midjourney then utilizes its AI algorithm to generate unique and visually appealing results.
- Varied artistic styles: The platform allows the generation of artwork in diverse artistic styles, ranging from photorealistic to abstract, impressionistic, and dreamlike.
- Iterative refinement: Users can refine their prompts based on the generated images, guiding the AI toward their desired outcome through a cycle of prompts and revisions.
- Community interaction: Midjourney operates within the Discord chat app, fostering a strong user community where artists can share prompts, discuss techniques, and provide feedback.

Who uses it:

- Artists and designers: Explore artistic concepts, generate variations on existing ideas, and create unique visual assets for creative projects.
- Writers and storytellers: Bring their narratives to life by visualizing scenes and characters.
- Entrepreneurs and marketers: Create unique and eye-catching visuals for branding, advertising, and social media.
- Anyone curious about AI-generated art: Experiment with the technology and discover its creative potential.

Benefits:

- Accessibility: Operates within Discord, requiring no specific coding knowledge or expensive software.
- Wide range of styles: Cater to diverse artistic preferences and project needs.
- Iterative approach: Allows for refining results and achieving greater creative control.
- Community and learning: Benefit from shared knowledge and insights within the Discord community.

So, you can create any image with Midjouney. Midjourney also gives you the commercial license for the image that you create. It means that you can use the image for whatever you want.

2. Recraft

Recraft is an AI-powered design platform launched in May 2022, aiming to empower professional designers and individuals with creative vision to effortlessly generate and refine visual content.

Here's a breakdown of Recraft's key features and uses:

Capabilities:

- Image generation: Create unique design elements like logos, icons, illustrations, vector graphics, and 3D models based on textual descriptions or reference images.
- Style transfer: Apply different artistic styles to existing images, experimenting with diverse creative directions.
- Image editing tools: Refine and enhance generated images with tools like background removal, color editing, object manipulation, and more.
- Vectorize images: Convert raster images (e.g., photos) into clean and scalable vector graphics.
- Collaborative workspaces: Invite others to collaborate on your projects and iterate on designs together.

Who can benefit:

- Graphic designers: Streamline workflows, explore creative options, and generate unique design assets rapidly.
- Marketers and advertisers: Create eye-catching visuals for branding, social media, and other marketing materials.

- Content creators: Generate visual elements for blog posts, videos, articles, and social media content.
- Individuals: Unleash your creativity for personal projects, design invitations, or explore art generation.

Key highlights:

- User-friendly interface: Designed for ease of use, even for those without design experience.
- Freemium model: Basic features are free, with paid plans offering advanced tools and unlimited usage.
- Growing community: Offers a forum for sharing creations, tutorials, and feedback.
- Constant evolution: New features and tools are regularly added.

Overall, Recraft.ai presents a valuable tool for individuals and professionals alike to explore the potential of AI in design. Whether you're looking to streamline your workflow, experiment with creative ideas, or simply generate unique visuals, Recraft might be worth checking out!

3. Suno AI

Suno AI is a fascinating tool utilizing artificial intelligence to democratize music creation. Launched in 2023, it empowers individuals of all musical backgrounds to generate unique songs by simply providing text prompts. Here's a breakdown of Suno AI's key features and potential:

Core Functionality:

- Turn text into music: Users input text descriptions outlining desired song characteristics like mood, genre, instruments, lyrics, or even specific musical references. Suno AI's AI model generates original melodic and harmonic structures based on the information provided.
- Refine and iterate: Unlike a static output, Suno allows users to refine specific sections of the generated music, adjusting elements like melody, instrumentation, or overall arrangement. This iterative process fosters a level of creative control for users.
- Multiple features: Besides generating songs, Suno offers additional features like generating sound effects, background music, and even simple vocals based on provided lyrics.

Who can benefit:

- Musicians and songwriters: Break through writer's block, explore new musical ideas, or quickly prototype song concepts.
- Content creators: Generate unique music for videos, podcasts, games, or other multimedia projects.

- Hobbyists and music enthusiasts: Experiment with music creation, learn about musical structures, and have fun exploring soundscapes.

Advantages:

- Accessibility: No prior musical knowledge is required, opening music creation to a wider audience.
- Speed and efficiency: Generate song ideas quickly, saving time and effort compared to traditional methods.
- Exploration and experimentation: Discover new musical possibilities and push creative boundaries.

Overall, Suno AI represents an exciting step forward in democratizing music creation. Whether you're a seasoned musician or simply curious about musical exploration, it offers a unique and accessible platform to explore the intersection of AI and music.

Now you know about the different types of AI tools. AI tools can help you in different ways, such as researching, writing, summarizing, creating images, and creating sound and music. These are only a few AI tools that I use frequently. If you need an AI tool for a specific job, just google it. It has many AI tools that can help you finish your job.

Now, let's look at ideas for using these AI tools to help you make money online easily.

How to Make Money Online With AI

I will show you 10 ways to make money online with AI in this topic. These methods are suitable for beginners to get started as soon as possible.

Blogging

AI can be a powerful tool for bloggers looking to increase efficiency, improve content quality, and generate income. Here's a breakdown of how you can leverage AI in your blogging journey:

Content Creation & Curation:

- Use AI writing assistants: Generate drafts, outlines, blog post intros and outros, or even full articles based on your prompts. Edit and fact-check before publishing.
- Content research and brainstorming: Use AI tools to find relevant statistics, quotes, and interesting facts.
- Personalize content for different audiences: AI can help tailor your writing style and tone to different demographics or customer segments.
- Curate content from other sources: AI tools can suggest relevant articles and resources to complement your content.

SEO & Marketing Optimization:

- Keyword research and optimizing: AI Tools can help you identify the ideas of keywords that have high search traffic and optimize your content for search engines.

- Social media content creation and scheduling: Use AI tools to analyze your social media posts and create new posts.

Monetization Strategies:

- Affiliate marketing: Promote relevant products or services within your content and earn commission on sales through your affiliate links.
- Display advertising: Use platforms like Google AdSense or Media.net to display targeted ads on your blog and earn revenue per click or impression.
- Paid memberships or exclusive content: Offer exclusive content, early access, or community features to paying subscribers through platforms.
- Sell your products or services: Leverage your audience to sell eBooks, courses, coaching, or other digital products related to your expertise.

Conclusion:

Creating content on your blog or website will no longer be difficult because AI can help you with keyword research, thinking of article titles, SEO, and creating images for the articles. All you need to do is use AI to create more and more articles. Then, make money from it using the method mentioned above.

Writing Books

While AI can't write an entire book independently, it can be a valuable tool for authors looking to streamline processes, spark creativity, and increase their chances of success. Here are some ways you can leverage AI to make money by writing books:

Content Creation and Development:

- Brainstorming and outlining: Use AI tools to generate ideas, create outlines, and develop plot points.
- Research and background information: AI Tools can help you find relevant statistics, quotes, and information for your book.
- Generating first drafts or specific sections: Explore AI to kickstart your writing process or tackle specific chapters.
- Character development and dialogue: AI Tools can help you brainstorm character traits motivations, and even generate realistic dialogue.

Editing and Polishing:

- Grammar and spell check: Utilize AI-powered platforms like Grammarly to catch errors and improve your writing style.
- Fact-checking and consistency: AI Tools can help you verify information and maintain consistency throughout your book.

Marketing and Publication:

- Keyword research and SEO optimization: Leverage AI tools to identify relevant keywords and optimize your book title, blurb, and metadata for search engines.
- Book cover design and formatting: Explore AI-powered design tools like Midjourney or Recraft to create unique and eye-catching book covers and format your manuscript for various platforms.

Additional Income Streams:

- Sell self-published eBooks: Leverage platforms like Amazon Kindle Direct Publishing or Kobo Writing Life to distribute your AI-assisted book directly and earn royalties.
- Offer audiobook versions: Utilize AI narration to convert your text into audiobooks and expand your reach to new audiences.
- Develop merchandise: Generate ideas and use AI-powered design tools to create branded merchandise related to your book content.

Conclusion:

Remember, success in writing relies on your passion, storytelling skills, and dedication to crafting a compelling narrative. However, AI can be a powerful ally in streamlining your workflow, overcoming writer's block, and reaching a wider audience.

Stock Photos

Generating stock photos with AI presents an intriguing avenue for earning income. While still evolving, this market holds potential for creative individuals and tech-savvy users. Here's how you can leverage AI to create and sell stock photos:

AI Tools for Photo Creation:

- Midjourney: Generates hyper-realistic and stylistic images based on detailed text prompts. Great for unique landscapes, objects, and abstract concepts.
- DALL-E 2: Offers similar capabilities to Midjourney, with strengths in photorealistic images and intricate details. Currently closed access but seeking beta testers.
- Artbreeder: Utilizes a "genetic" approach, allowing you to blend and evolve existing images to create unique variations. Ideal for artistic and experimental styles.
- NightCafe Creator: Leverages various AI models for diverse artistic styles and photorealism. Offers both free and paid options.

Considerations for AI-Generated Stock Photos:

- Quality and originality: Aim for high-resolution, visually appealing images that stand out. Experiment with diverse prompts and refine your creations.
- Legal aspects: Ensure your AI tool allows commercial use and clearly state any usage limitations in your licensing agreements.

- Keyword optimization: Use relevant keywords in your image titles, descriptions, and tags to improve discoverability on stock photo platforms.

Monetization Strategies:

- Stock photo marketplaces: Submit your photos to established platforms like Adobe Stock or Getty Images. Each platform has its own submission requirements and commission rates.
- Microstock platforms: Consider platforms like 123RF or Dreamstime, offering lower entry barriers and potentially higher royalty rates for niche content.
- Subscription services: Create a subscription-based service offering exclusive access to your AI-generated content libraries.

Remember:

- Quality and creativity are key: Despite AI assistance, focus on delivering visually stunning and engaging images that cater to specific market needs.
- Ethical considerations: Be mindful of potential biases in AI models and avoid generating harmful or offensive content.
- Transparency and disclosure: Clearly state how your photos were created and adhere to licensing agreements responsibly.

Conclusion:

While the AI stock photo market is still emerging, it offers exciting opportunities for those willing to experiment, hone their skills, and leverage technology creatively. With a strategic approach and dedication to quality, you can make income by turning your AI-powered visions into marketable images.

Photo Editor

AI is rapidly transforming the photo editing landscape, offering exciting new ways to monetize your skills and creativity. Here's a detailed breakdown of various methods:

AI-Assisted Photo Editing Services:

- Offer editing for photographers: Partner with photographers who need help with bulk editing, background removal, object manipulation, or enhancing specific aspects like color correction. Master AI tools like Luminar AI, Topaz Labs, and Adobe Photoshop to deliver professional results efficiently.
- Freelance editing for businesses: Businesses increasingly use visuals for marketing and advertising. Offer AI-powered photo editing services for product photos, social media content, and website images. Highlight your ability to create consistent styles and meet tight deadlines.
- Specialized editing niches: Focus on specific areas like portrait retouching, real estate photo enhancement, or wedding photo editing. Develop expertise in the relevant AI tools and cater to the unique needs of your chosen niche.

Hybrid Approach:

- Combine AI with traditional editing: Don't entirely replace traditional editing skills with AI. Use AI tools to automate repetitive tasks, but retain your creative vision and manual editing skills for fine-tuning and achieving the desired results.

- Offer a tiered service: Provide different service levels with varying degrees of AI involvement. This caters to clients with different budgets and preferences, offering affordable AI-assisted editing and premium handcrafted edits.

Conclusion:

By understanding these methods and leveraging your creativity and AI skills, you can unlock new opportunities to make money with photo editing in the exciting world of AI-powered image manipulation.

Selling Prompt

The rise of AI tools like image generators and content creators has opened up a unique opportunity: selling prompts to monetize your creativity and understanding of these systems. Here's a breakdown of different approaches:

Prompt Marketplaces:

- Dedicated platforms: Explore marketplaces like PromptBase, Hugging Face Hub, or PromptHero, specifically designed for buying and selling prompts. Many cater to AI tools like Midjourney, DALL-E, or GPT-3.
- Freelance platforms: Utilize Fiverr, Upwork, or Etsy to offer prompt creation services. Target clients are seeking assistance with specific content generation tasks or artistic styles.

Niche-Specific Prompts:

- Focus on specific creative fields: Cater to specific niches like graphic design, marketing, advertising, or writing. Develop prompts tailored to their needs, like product descriptions, blog post ideas, or social media captions.
- Target professional industries: Offer prompts for legal documents, medical reports, or financial analysis tailored to professionals in those fields. Ensure accuracy and compliance with relevant regulations.

Pre-generated Prompt Packs:

- Create themed packs: Bundle prompts around themes like fantasy landscapes, science fiction characters, or historical scenarios. Sell them on your website, through stock photo platforms, or marketplaces.

- Offer niche-specific packs: Develop prompt packs targeting specific industries or creative needs, like product mockups, social media ad templates, or email marketing prompts.

Value-Added Services:

- Combine prompts with tutorials: Offer prompts and tutorials on using them effectively with different AI tools. Cater to beginners or those unfamiliar with specific platforms.
- Provide prompt customization: Clients can request personalized prompts based on their needs and preferences. Offer consultations or customization packages for additional value.
- Curated prompt collections: Assembled and curated collections of high-performing prompts for specific purposes, like generating realistic portraits, creating artistic compositions, or writing different creative content formats.

Conclusion:

By understanding these strategies and focusing on quality, niche expertise, and value-added services, you can unlock the potential of selling prompts and make money in this exciting new market driven by AI creativity.

Selling POD

Print-on-demand (POD) offers a flexible way to sell physical products without upfront inventory costs. Combining POD with AI opens exciting opportunities to create unique designs and reach wider audiences. Here's a detailed breakdown:

AI-Generated Designs:

- Leverage AI image generators: Utilize tools like Midjourney to create original artwork for your POD products. Offer designs tailored to specific niches like fantasy art, abstract patterns, or trending styles.
- Experiment with AI text-to-image tools: Explore platforms like Imagen or Dream by WOMBO to translate text descriptions into unique visuals. Translate popular quotes, inspirational messages, or funny slogans into eye-catching designs.
- Combine AI with manual editing: Don't rely solely on AI. Use it to generate ideas and variations, then enhance them with your design skills and editing software to ensure quality and originality.

Niche-Specific Designs:

- Focus on targeted audiences: Identify specific niches with passionate communities, like pet lovers, gamers, or sports fans. Create designs based on their interests and inside jokes to resonate with them deeply.
- Partner with niche communities: Collaborate with influencers, bloggers, or online groups within your chosen niche. Create designs based on their content or inside jokes, offering them a share of the profits.

Data-Driven Design Choices:

- Analyze POD platform trends: Use AI to utilize sales data and platform insights to identify popular design elements, color palettes, and product categories in your chosen niche. Adapt your designs based on this data to increase appeal and sales potential.
- Use social media analytics: Use AI to analyze which types of visual content perform well on social media platforms relevant to your target audience. Use this data to inform your design choices and marketing strategies.

Remember:

- Quality matters: Ensure your designs are high-resolution, visually appealing, and relevant to your target audience. Don't compromise on quality due to AI shortcuts.
- Marketing is key: Utilize social media, content marketing, and targeted advertising to reach your ideal customers. Showcase your unique designs and the value you offer.
- Experiment and adapt: Be willing to experiment with different design styles, niches, and POD platforms. Analyze your results and adapt your strategies based on what performs best.

Conclusion:

By harnessing the power of AI while focusing on quality, niche expertise, and value-added services, you can unlock the potential of POD and build a successful business selling unique and in-demand products.

Marketing Consultant

AI is transforming the marketing landscape, and marketing consultants can leverage this by offering specialized services and knowledge to clients. Here's an exploration of different approaches:

AI-Powered Marketing Audits & Strategy:

- Analyze marketing data with AI: Utilize AI tools to analyze vast amounts of customer data, social media engagement, and marketing campaign performance. Offer clients data-driven insights and recommendations for optimizing strategies.
- Develop AI-powered marketing personas: Use AI tools to analyze customer behavior and build detailed personas based on demographics, interests, and online activity. Help clients understand their target audience better for more effective marketing.
- Predict marketing trends with AI: Leverage AI tools to analyze market trends, competitor strategies, and social media buzz. Offer clients insights into future trends and opportunities to stay ahead of the curve.

Implementing AI Marketing Tools & Techniques:

- Set up and manage AI-powered ad campaigns: Help clients implement and manage AI-powered advertising platforms like Google Ads or Facebook Ads. Optimize campaigns for targeting, bidding, and creative content using AI insights.
- Integrate chatbots and AI assistants: Assist clients in implementing AI-powered chatbots for customer service

or lead generation. Train the bots and manage their performance to improve customer experience and conversions.

- Personalize marketing content with AI: Utilize AI tools like copywriting assistants or content recommendations to personalize marketing materials and website content for individual customers. Increase engagement and conversion rates.

Training & Education on AI Marketing:

- Conduct workshops and training sessions: Offer workshops or training sessions for businesses on understanding and using AI for marketing purposes. Teach them to analyze data, choose the right tools, and implement effective strategies.
- Develop online courses on AI marketing: Create and sell online courses on various aspects of AI marketing, like using AI tools, analyzing data, or building AI-powered campaigns. Cater to different levels of expertise.
- Write educational content and blog posts: Share your knowledge and insights by writing blog posts, articles, or eBooks on AI marketing trends, best practices, and case studies. Establish yourself as an expert and attract potential clients.

Niche Expertise in Specific AI Tools or Industries:

- Become an expert in specific AI marketing tools: Deepen your knowledge in tools like Google Marketing Platform, HubSpot AI, or Adobe Sensei. Offer specialized consulting services for clients who want to maximize the use of these platforms.
- Focus on specific industries: Develop expertise in applying AI marketing to healthcare, finance, or e-commerce. Cater your services to businesses within these industries, highlighting your targeted knowledge.

Conclusion:

By embracing AI and developing specialized knowledge, marketing consultants can unlock new opportunities to deliver valuable services, stay ahead of the curve, and build successful businesses in the ever-evolving marketing landscape.

Making Music

AI is transforming the music industry, offering exciting ways to create, collaborate, and monetize your musical talents. Here's a comprehensive breakdown of different approaches:

AI-Assisted Composition and Production:

- Compose with AI tools: Utilize tools like Amper Music, MuseNet, or Jukebox to generate musical ideas, melodies, and harmonies. Refine them with your musical knowledge and craft unique compositions.
- Produce music with AI loops and samples: Leverage AI-powered sample packs or loop libraries to create professional-sounding productions. Add your instruments, vocals, and editing skills to personalize them.
- Offer AI-powered music production services: Partner with musicians, singers, or composers who need help with specific production tasks like beat creation, sound design, or arrangement. Utilize AI tools to streamline your workflow and offer efficient services.

AI-Generated Content Creation:

- Create AI-powered soundtracks and jingles: Develop royalty-free soundtracks for video games, apps, or advertisements using AI tools. Sell them through stock music platforms or directly to clients.
- Compose AI-powered musical NFTs: Experiment with generative AI platforms to create unique and original music NFTs. Offer them on dedicated NFT marketplaces catering to music enthusiasts.

- Develop personalized music experiences: Utilize AI to generate music based on user preferences, moods, or activities. Offer this as a subscription service or integrated into existing music apps.

Education and Training on AI Music:

- Teach musicians how to use AI tools: Offer workshops, online courses, or tutorials on using AI for music creation, production, or composition. Share your knowledge and expertise to empower others.
- Develop educational resources on AI music: Create eBooks, video tutorials, or blog posts on various aspects of AI music, like choosing the right tools, mastering specific workflows, or exploring creative applications.

Hybrid Approach:

- Combine AI with traditional music production: Don't entirely replace your musical skills with AI. Use AI tools for inspiration, generating ideas, or automating repetitive tasks. Focus your creativity on crafting unique melodies and arrangements and adding your personal touch.

Conclusion:

By understanding these methods and creatively leveraging your musical skills and AI tools, you can unlock exciting opportunities to make money and share your unique voice in the ever-evolving world of AI-powered music.

Selling Game Assets

AI is becoming a powerful tool in game development, and creating and selling game assets is one way to leverage this technology for financial gain. Here's a detailed breakdown of different approaches:

AI-Assisted Asset Creation:

Generate base models with AI: Utilize tools like Artbreeder or Midjourney to create unique 3D models, environments, or textures. Refine them in traditional 3D modeling software and ensure they meet game engine compatibility standards.

Use AI for specific tasks: Leverage AI tools for repetitive tasks like generating variations of an object, creating textures based on existing patterns, or procedurally generating landscapes.

Offer AI-assisted asset creation services: Partner with game developers who need help generating base models or variations of existing assets. Combine your AI knowledge with 3D modeling skills to deliver high-quality results.

Specialized AI-Generated Assets:

Focus on niche assets: Create unique AI-generated assets for specific game genres or styles, like hand-painted textures for indie games or photorealistic props for realistic simulations.

Develop procedural generation tools: Utilize your AI expertise to create tools that developers can use to generate their in-game assets based on specific parameters. Sell these tools on asset marketplaces or directly to studios.

Offer AI-powered character customization options: Develop systems that allow players to personalize their characters using AI-generated variations of hairstyles, clothing, or facial features. Sell these systems to game developers seeking unique customization options.

Traditional Assets with AI Enhancements:

Combine AI with manual creation: Use AI for specific aspects of your asset creation workflow, like generating initial concepts, exploring color palettes, or adding procedural details. Focus your skills on refining the assets for quality and game engine compatibility.

Offer AI-powered optimization services: Partner with developers who need help optimizing their existing assets for performance or specific platforms. Utilize AI tools to streamline this process and deliver efficient solutions.

Education and Training:

Teach game developers how to use AI tools: Offer workshops, online courses, or tutorials on using AI for game asset creation. Share your knowledge and expertise to empower others in the industry.

Develop educational resources on AI for games: Create eBooks, video tutorials, or blog posts on various aspects of AI in game development, including asset creation, optimization, and best practices.

Remember:

- Quality and game-readiness are paramount: Ensure your assets are high-quality, visually appealing, and optimized for the target game engine. Don't compromise on quality due to AI shortcuts.
- Target the right audience: Understand the needs of your ideal game developers and create assets that cater to specific genres, styles, or technical requirements.
- Market your assets effectively: Showcase your work on asset marketplaces, your website, or relevant online communities. Utilize targeted marketing strategies to reach potential buyers.

Conclusion:

By understanding these methods, leveraging your creativity and AI skills strategically, and focusing on quality and niche expertise, you can unlock new opportunities to make money by selling game assets in the exciting world of AI-powered game development.

Creating Online Course

AI is transforming the landscape of online learning, offering exciting ways to create, deliver, and monetize your expertise. Here's a detailed breakdown of different approaches to utilize AI in creating online courses:

AI-Assisted Course Creation:

- Generate content outlines and ideas: Use AI tools like ShortlyAI or Jasper to brainstorm topic ideas, create outlines, and draft initial content for your course modules. Refine them with your subject matter expertise and ensure accuracy.
- Develop interactive elements with AI: Leverage tools like Quizlet or Nearpod to create engaging quizzes, polls, and interactive activities for your learners. AI can personalize these based on individual progress for a more dynamic learning experience.
- Personalize course content with AI: Utilize AI-powered recommendation engines to personalize learning paths and suggest relevant additional resources based on individual student needs and progress.

AI-Powered Course Production & Delivery:

- Use AI for video editing and animation: Tools like Descript or RunwayML can automate basic editing tasks and even create explainer animations, saving time and resources. Ensure the final output aligns with your overall course style and branding.
- Implement AI-powered chatbots and virtual assistants: Integrate chatbots to answer student questions, provide

support, and offer personalized guidance within your course. This can improve student engagement and satisfaction.

- Offer AI-graded assessments: Use AI-powered grading tools for multiple-choice questions or essay prompts, freeing your time for personalized feedback and student interactions.

AI-Enhanced Marketing & Promotion:

- Optimize course descriptions and metadata with AI: Use AI tools to analyze keywords and optimize your course descriptions and metadata for better search engine visibility and organic reach.
- Create targeted ads with AI: Leverage AI-powered advertising platforms to reach your ideal audience with personalized ad campaigns based on demographics, interests, and online behavior.
- Analyze student data with AI: Utilize AI to analyze student engagement, completion rates, and feedback to identify areas for improvement and refine your course content and delivery methods.

Unique AI-Focused Courses:

- Develop courses on using AI for specific fields: Teach students how to use AI tools for graphic design, writing, marketing, or other relevant industries. Offer your unique expertise and insights in this emerging field.
- Create courses on the ethical implications of AI: Explore the societal and ethical considerations surrounding AI development and applications. Offer a critical

perspective and guide students through responsible AI use.

- Build AI-powered simulations for training: Develop interactive simulations powered by AI that allow learners to practice real-world scenarios and hone their skills in a safe and engaging environment.

Remember:

- Focus on quality and value: Ensure your courses are well-structured, informative, and provide practical value to learners. Don't rely solely on AI for content creation. Prioritize quality and accuracy.
- Target the right audience: Understand your ideal student persona and tailor your content, marketing, and pricing accordingly.
- Stay updated on AI trends: The AI landscape evolves rapidly. Keep your knowledge current and integrate new advancements into your course content and delivery methods.
- Combine AI with your expertise: Don't replace your teaching skills with AI. Utilize AI tools to enhance your workflow, personalize learning experiences, and offer a unique and valuable learning experience.

Conclusion:

By understanding these methods and leveraging your expertise and AI tools strategically, you can unlock new opportunities to create high-quality, engaging online courses and build a successful business in the ever-evolving world of AI-powered education.

Launching Your AI-Powered Journey

Congratulations on reaching the end of this exploration into the exciting world of making money online with AI! You now have a solid understanding of generative AI, some excellent AI tool recommendations, and ten diverse pathways to explore your entrepreneurial spirit. Remember, this is just the beginning. The true adventure lies in taking action and applying what you've learned.

Fueling the Fire with Action:

Before you dive headfirst, take a moment to reflect on your strengths, interests, and resources. Which of the ten methods resonated most with you? Do you have existing skills you can leverage, or are you eager to embark on a new learning journey?

Remember, success rarely happens overnight. Be patient, consistent, and adaptable. Start small, experiment, and refine your approach based on feedback and results. Embrace the learning curve – it's part of the exciting journey!

Your AI Arsenal:

Let's revisit the AI tools we discussed:

- For text generation: ChatGPT, Gemini, Bing Copilot
- For image manipulation: Midjourney, Recraft
- For music composition: Suno AI

Remember, this is just a starting point. Explore, research, and find the tools best suit your needs and budget.

Beyond the Tools:

While AI is a powerful tool, it's crucial to remember it's a collaborative partner, not a magic wand. Your human touch, creativity, and strategic thinking are irreplaceable. Focus on providing value, solving problems, and building genuine connections with your audience.

Remember:

- Stay ethical and responsible in your AI usage. Be transparent about its involvement and respect intellectual property rights.
- Embrace the community. Connect with other AI enthusiasts, learn from their experiences, and share your journey.
- Never stop learning. The AI landscape constantly evolves, so stay updated on the latest trends and advancements.

This is not goodbye, but rather a "see you soon" as you embark on your AI-powered journey. As you navigate the exciting online business world, remember the lessons learned in this book, embrace the challenges, and celebrate your successes.

The future is full of possibilities, and with the power of AI at your fingertips, you have the potential to achieve amazing things. Now, go forth and make your mark in the world!

Buck Tyler

Buck Tyler isn't your average Joe. He's traded the traditional office grind for the freedom of the open road, making waves in the digital nomad scene for over a decade. With a laptop for his office and the world as his canvas, Buck has mastered the art of online income generation, exploring various pathways from affiliate marketing to mobile app development, online courses, website building, and even writing novels.